PARENT PROMISES

12 Promises to Give Your Child Strength for Life

Janet R. Geisz, M.A.

VANTAGE PRESS
New York

To my children

FIRST EDITION

All rights reserved, including the right of
reproduction in whole or in part in any form.

Copyright © 2001 by Janet R. Geisz, M.A.

Published by Vantage Press, Inc.
516 West 34th Street, New York, New York 10001

Manufactured in the United States of America
ISBN: 0-533-13580-X

Library of Congress Catalog Card No.: 00-91495

0 9 8 7 6 5 4 3 2 1

Contents

Introduction   v

I.	I Promise You Absolute Love	3
II.	I Promise to Be a Responsible Parent	13
III.	I Promise to Make You a Top Priority	21
IV.	I Promise You My Time	27
V.	I Promise to Listen to You	35
VI.	I Promise to Accept and Respect You for Who You Are	41
VII.	I Promise to Be Honest with You	49
VIII.	I Promise to Guide You by Setting a Good Example	55
IX.	I Promise to Set Appropriate Limits	63
X.	I Promise to Be Patient	71
XI.	I Promise to Protect You	79
XII.	I Promise to Help You Develop Independence	85

Final Comments   91
Bibliography   95

Introduction

Wait! There is no simple formula for raising perfect, problem-free children. There is no magic recipe for "perfect" parenting. However, there are ways to give our children emotional and spiritual well-being, through ***honorable interactions.*** Honorable interactions create bonds of mutual trust and respect that strengthen children and help prepare them to handle the challenges of life.

There are certain ways of relating to children, even children with severe problems, that will help increase their chances of being confident, competent, and caring individuals—children who are responsible, productive, and noble members of our society. Regardless of their individual assets and limitations, there are ways more likely to secure the future for your children, by embracing them with honorable interactions.

In this country we know many of our precious children are suffering. We know this because we are witnessing consistent increases in childhood depression, anger, detachment, underachievement, self-destruction, and disrespect. We see the effects of this in our homes, our schools, and our communities. The number of children on mood or behavior-altering medications is steadily increasing. Yet, we also see that many children are thriving in our society, many are still happy, enthusiastic, and talented. This is because children can still be pleasant and charming to be around if cherished by the important adults in their lives.

Professionals working with children who have learning problems or behavior problems have learned that any child's problem can be greatly magnified or greatly minimized by the quality of adult interactions with that child. Most children with severe problems do not need to have as many problems as they do. Many of the difficulties could be prevented or at least minimized with the right adult attention and intervention at the right time. Adult input at home, at school, and in the community all influence the degree of difficulties faced by children. We would not be seeing so many insecure, out of shape, unhappy, out of control, even threatening, young people if they were getting what they need from the adults around them.

All loving parents want what's right for their children. At the same time parents are often confused about how to even identify, much less be sure of, what's right for their children. Most parents seem to know that a child's development results from complex interactions between the child's innate attributes and a lifetime of experiences. We know environmental circumstances impact the child emotionally, cognitively, and spiritually. Even if we think we know what is right for our children as parents, we cannot control all environmental circumstances that will influence them. Parents can become overwhelmed by the prospect that so much of what affects their child in the environment is beyond their control. It is true we cannot always control every outside exposure or a child's reactions to life. Still, parents need to realize they do have great power to influence how their children develop.

To gain the power to influence we have to look at what we are really doing to, or for, our children on the basic levels of interaction. Although we all want what's best for our children, it is too often not being provided, even at home where we have the most control. Even in families that would appear to have all the advantages, often children are not getting what they need. We see suffering children in intact two-parent homes as well as in single-parent homes; in affluent homes as well as in economically deprived homes; in homes with strong religious activity as well as in homes with little or no religious activity. Although strong family, spiritual, and financial security assuredly do help, children from all different backgrounds can live in high conflict or over-stressed homes where they do not get the support, time, guidance, nurturing, mentoring, and modeling they need from adults. It is imperative that parents identify and then concentrate on what they personally can do to increase their child's chances of well-being.

Too many children grow up suffering because of inadequate relationships with adults. We cannot afford to continue to let this happen because it affects all of us and will cause problems way into the future. We all have a stake in how children turn out. To help strengthen our children we all must get a better understanding of what they need to succeed. We need to prevent childhood problems by giving our children the attention and support they need from early in life and throughout their developing years. Every adult in this country should take some responsibility to have a positive influence on children, even if only by setting an example of honor, morality, dignity, and respect for others. Parents, especially, have an obligation to find effective ways to support and encourage healthy, well-rounded development in their children.

In order to thrive every child has to be guaranteed certain rights of humane treatment, especially by a loving parent. This humane treatment begins with having honorable interactions. All parents should be willing to make certain promises regarding how they will relate to their children, in order to help them flourish. No law will require parents to make such promises. In fact, as vital as effective parenting is to our future, there are no formal requirements to meet any exemplary standards of parental conduct, no requirement for commitment to excellence. There are not even any required preparations for the job of parenting.

Most people are left with trying to parent the way they were parented, modified by living with much more complex challenges to values and more demands on our time than our own parent models experienced. Also, much of what we learn about being a parent comes from on-the-job-training, including trial and error. The problem is that on-the-job training takes time and as we learn from our mistakes, our children are affected by our mistakes. Most children will survive anyway, with only mild to moderate suffering. But, do we want our children to just survive or do we want them to thrive?

Fortunately, to improve their chances of success, devoted parents seek information and training on their own. From a mountain of varied material, we are offered plenty of information and several different methods to explore that can help us parent. For years searching parents have been bombarded by conflicting advice about how to deal with the complexities of raising children. Luckily, there are several pathways to success. No single method offers all the answers.

This book is not meant to provide all that parents need to know about raising children. It is not an all-inclusive parenting manual. It is meant to suggest that parents can strengthen their bonds with their children through honorable interactions. By keeping certain promises to your children, you can establish a stronger, more influential relationship. A relationship that will not only be enjoyable and rewarding to you as a parent but that will also strengthen your children by giving them lifelong survival tools. This book attempts to combine, clarify, and simplify the basic requirements of establishing a lasting, loving, and influential bond with your children through dignified and honorable interactions.

These basic requirements are presented in the form of twelve fundamental ***Parent Promises,*** that every parent can make to their children. Keeping these promises to your child will help you build better parent/child relationships and will benefit all aspects of your child's development. The twelve fundamental promises are listed on the following page. Then, each promise is discussed in more detail in one of the following chapters.

I. I Promise You Absolute Love.
II. I Promise to Be a Responsible Parent.
III. I Promise to Make You a Top Priority.
IV. I Promise You My Time.
V. I Promise to Listen to You.
VI. I Promise to Accept You and Respect You for Who You Are.
VII. I Promise to Be Honest with You.
VIII. I Promise to Guide You by Setting a Good Example.
IX. I Promise to Set Appropriate Limits.
X. I Promise to Be Patient.
XI. I Promise to Protect You.
XII. I Promise to Help You Develop Independence.

If each of these twelve promises is kept, you will be rewarded by having a trusting and loving relationship with your children throughout your life. This combination of promises will help you remember to relate to your children lovingly in ways that will support their development by providing for physical, emotional, cognitive, and spiritual well-being. They are essential promises needed in order to establish a high level of influence over your child's choices in life.

If you believe you have already made critical mistakes with your children, remember, no matter what has happened so far it is not too late to promise and give your children the needed support suggested in this book. Past mistakes don't have to dictate the future. ***A moment is not eternity, there is power in time.*** You have time to minimize the effects of previous mistakes by keeping these twelve promises in the future, thereby beginning the development of a lasting bond of mutual respect with your children.

By keeping these promises, you will enjoy raising your children. You will have the opportunity to live with their childlike wonder and enthusiasm. Happy children are energetic and fun to be around. Your effort, time, energy, and attention will greatly enhance your chances of successfully raising thriving children who are confident, competent, caring, responsible, productive, and honorable. Children who will, in return, treat you with dignity and respect over your lifetime. Remember, the quality of your ongoing relationships with your children will also determine how much influence you will have with them throughout the years.

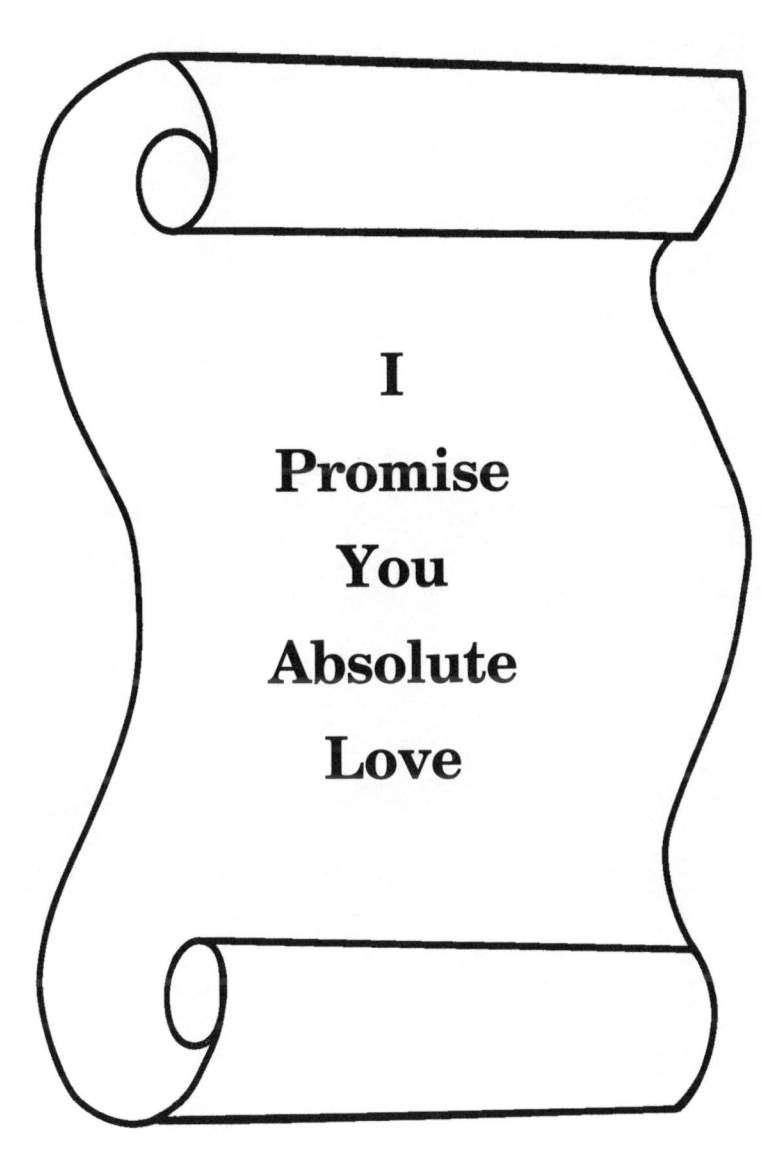

I

I Promise You Absolute Love

A parent's love illuminates a child's soul, if the love is absolute and without stipulation. In an unconditionally loving environment, your child's natural enthusiasm for life will thrive. Your child's inherent abilities will blossom.

All children are lovable, and all parents love their children. Right? So why don't all children feel loved? Why don't they all thrive and blossom? Why are we seeing so many children who are in serious trouble? Why are the needs of so many children not being met? How can parents' love be more supportive of their children? How can parents demonstrate their love more effectively, so that it is realized by their children?

First of all, it is a mistake to assume that your children will just automatically know how loved they are by all the things you do for them every day, especially if these things require you being off and gone too often. Love must be demonstrated directly to children. They need to concretely experience something to really know it and believe it. Young children need to be frequently cuddled and coddled by loving parents. They need to be told how much you appreciate their uniqueness. Our children need to know we find them remarkable.

Making sure your child feels loved every day is your most important job as a parent. The groundwork for your child's emotional well-being will be established in her first years of life. The main requirement for a child's emotional health is to feel loved. Your child's self-esteem, how she deals with other people, and how she views the world in general, will be based, to a large extent, on how lovable she believes herself to be. For a child, the first and most influential examples of how lovable she is will come from her parents. The loving relationship established between you and your child will help determine the kind of love relationships that she will have throughout her life.

Even a child's brain development is somewhat dependent on loving treatment. The developing brain is responsive to everything it experiences. Everything your baby experiences causes chemical and electrical activities in the developing brain to create neural impulses and establish permanent connections and brain patterns. Your baby needs to be held and rocked in order to develop brain patterns for efficient learning. Tenderly holding and lovingly talking to your infant establishes a foundation for language development and communication skills that will affect all of her future learning.

Many parents believe they adequately demonstrate their love by providing for and caring for their children while keeping them safe, meeting basic human needs for nourishment and shelter. While having nourishment and shelter provides feelings of security, children need more than the basics to spiritually thrive. Parents must be physically available so their children can directly see, feel, and hear their parents' love. If both parents are spending too many hours away from their children, working to provide nourishment, shelter, and material pleasures, they may not have much time to actually be with their children to provide the physical cuddling and coddling as well as the verbal affirmations that are needed. Make sure you balance your life so you have time to hug, hold, kiss, and talk with your child frequently. These are the concrete examples of tenderness and love that all children need daily.

It is easy to give absolute, unconditional love to a tiny infant who totally depends on you and never challenges your authority. Later on, when children begin to have minds of their own and begin to talk back, the loving parent-child relationship becomes more complex. Issues of power and control crop up, requiring more from the parent than just nurturing. Parents who originally just wanted to be sweet and loving, often find themselves trying anything they can to win the power struggles. To show absolute love begins to require more than just nurturing.

As your child ages and your balancing act between authority and tenderness becomes more difficult, at times you will find yourself wanting to use all kinds of force (physical, verbal, or emotional) to gain control over the situation. Under stressful moments you will probably find yourself resorting to some of the same methods that your parents used on you when you were a child. But, no matter what the age of the child, parents do not need to resort to emotional blackmail to control their children. There can never be conditions that a child must meet, no strings attached, to get love from a parent. Demonstrations of your love should never be held back until your child pleases you or complies with your demands. Parental love must be given unconditionally, as a birthright offered to every child. Even in discipline, your goals to help your child learn responsibility and develop her potential will never require withdrawal of your loving behavior toward her.

Many parents are stressed with feelings of responsibility about properly training their children as soon as possible. They may even feel in competition with other parents to accomplish proper training in their children first. When you feel pressure to force adequate training, now(!), it may help to remember that children have several years to learn to be responsible and self-sufficient. Thankfully, they do not start out as miniature adults. It's a long, slow process. Through the developmental process children need to be assured of their parent's support, even if they make mistakes. Children who are confident, as they grow up, of their parent's unconditional love, are free to explore the world, learn from making mistakes, develop skills, and continually reach for developing their potential.

If you do not demonstrate unconditional love for your child, she may grow up feeling unworthy of love. She may feel she has to earn your love by pleasing you, which can lead to an overwhelming need to please others, including undesirable peers, adults, or partners. When a child has to spend her time and energy pleasing and performing for others in an effort to earn love, she may not be free to develop her own interests, talents, and abilities. While she tries to please, she may seem quite accomplished for a long time but may possibly be terribly unhappy inside. Eventually this unhappiness will express itself in some way. If she does not give up completely, your child may become obsessed with being perfect. She may be compulsive about her performance and unable to accept any defeat or failure. Being afraid to fail will limit what a person is willing to try and will stifle attempts at new learning and development of new skills.

If you were not fortunate enough to have been given unconditional love as a child, remember that as a parent you have a second chance at being part of a loving, nurturing, and supportive parent-child relationship, this time as the parent. Although most adults tend to parent the way they themselves were parented, all of us can learn to be a better parent. You can learn to demonstrate unconditional love to your own child even if you were not the recipient of this kind of love as a child.

Don't be too hard on yourself as a parent. All of us have to deal with challenges unique to our individual circumstances. All of us have times when we react to our children in ways that we later regret. All parents have times when they get angry at their children, but parents differ in how they handle the anger.

As you deal with your own child, think about the kind of treatment that makes you feel loved. Being controlled, examined, judged, criticized, pushed, suspected, threatened, guilt-tripped, pitied, or smothered does not feel loving. Being nurtured, accepted, respected, supported, encouraged, trusted, and appreciated make us feel loved and valued. These feelings help all of us better handle the challenges of life. Children are motivated to accomplish when they know they are loved and valued, no matter what their assets or limitations, and no matter what they have or have not done—absolutely and unconditionally loved by caring and compassionate parents.

II

I Promise to Be a Responsible Parent

Being a responsible parent is part of being a responsible adult. Responsible adults fulfill commitments and honor obligations. They make sure what is needed gets done without looking for excuses. They keep themselves able, able to handle life's challenges. They make sure they are ready before taking on new responsibilities.

Responsible parents recognize the serious demands of raising a child. Bringing a child into this world obligates you to nurture, encourage, guide and care for her for the next 18 to 20 years, and love her forever. This is an enormous commitment. The obligation includes devoting yourself, your attention, your energy, your time, and your money to providing for your child's needs. These needs vary through the years as the child develops; therefore the demands change. But for responsible parents there are always demands.

Being responsible does not mean being perfect. Perfect parenting is not possible or necessary. Have you ever met a perfect person? Trying to be a perfect parent will cause problems for you and everyone around you. To be responsible you will need to acknowledge your own limitations and moments of poor judgment. You will need to accept your mistakes and plan on learning from each one. Children can be quite resilient, and they will have many opportunities in life to recover from both their own and their parent's mistakes. If you take seriously your responsibilities as a parent and strive to do the right thing, you and your children will survive errors in judgment and misguided attempts.

By fulfilling your commitments and honoring your obligations as a parent, you will teach your children that you can be trusted. They will respect you and they will, as a result, learn to respect and trust others in authority. This will prevent a multitude of defiance problems that children, who have not learned to respect authority face at school and in the community.

Children are dependent on their parents for basic human needs. Parents have the responsibility to make sure their children eat healthy food, get plenty of sleep, and get adequate physical exercise. Only when these basic needs are met can children begin to reach their potential mentally, physically, and emotionally. In today's hectic world, it is challenging for even the most responsible parents to establish the healthy habits and routines for eating, sleeping, and exercising that every child needs. Responsible parents make sure it happens. If they need help in providing these basics for their children, then they get the help. If personal sacrifices are required, responsible parents make the sacrifices and make sure their children are properly cared for.

Parenting your child physically, emotionally, and spiritually is not a responsibility that you can completely turn over to someone else. You can't leave it up to your spouse and you can't hire it done. And you certainly can't exchange child care for child entertainment, plopping your children in front of the TV or a computer for hours, or signing them up for every outside activity available, in your absence.

You can get help caring for your child when you need it, but you cannot expect anyone you hire to fully take over or to give your child all the nurturing, guidance, and attention needed from a parent. Your children need you. Any time you spend positively interacting with your young child will prevent hours of difficulty in the more challenging years of adolescence.

If caring for and interacting with your child does not fit into your lifestyle, to make it fit you'll have to change your lifestyle. You will have to build in flexibility and time for mountains of patience. Some would-be parents should reconsider having a child before they take on the responsibility, if they are not willing to make lifestyle changes that are required to accommodate their child's needs.

As a responsible parent, you cannot allow your personal addictions to dominate your life and still be available to your children. An addiction means being a slave to a habit that interferes with balanced functioning. This does not only include addictions to drugs. People can be addicted to a job, success, power, sex, money, shopping, sports, television, eating, exercising, church activities, politics, socializing, personal fulfillment, volunteering, pleasing others, etc. Being a slave to any pursuit will detract from your ability to meet your obligations in raising your children and responding to their needs.

However, being a responsible parent does not require you to become a slave to your child either. Too much catering to a child's every demand will be just as damaging as any other addiction. With attention to experience, you will learn to recognize the difference between your child's needs and her wants. You won't have the energy to be a responsible parent unless you take care of your own needs also. A healthy balance in your life, including a variety of interests, obligations, and joys when combined to establish your own mental, emotional, and physical well-being, will allow you to be the kind of parent that your children need. You will also be the kind of role model they need. You will be showing them how a person establishes a healthy balance in life, so they will be able to do so for the rest of their lives.

Responsible parents model responsible behavior for their children. Parents cannot put their own desires above the needs of everyone else. Responsible parents live by the values of their spirituality, say what they mean, and behave accordingly. They follow the rules of society or work to change them. They make mistakes but they accept accountability for their mistakes without blaming others. They solve problems without destroying relationships.

All children need responsible parents in order to have their needs met sufficiently. Children need the security that a responsible parent provides, and they also need the example that a responsible parent provides. The best way to get your child to be responsible, to be accountable, and to be able to problem-solve effectively is to live this way yourself. Your example of being responsible is your child's earliest and most influential teacher.

III

I Promise to Make You a Top Priority

The moment you become a parent, your most important job becomes ***parenting.*** Since you decided to bring a child into the world, you have an obligation to provide your child with what he needs to develop into a worthwhile individual. What could be more important than raising your child to become a person who is an asset to mankind? Helping him develop into a responsible, compassionate, honorable person must become one of your top priorities as the parent.

Adults today are offered countless opportunities for challenge, personal growth, excitement, and entertainment. It's hard to turn down these opportunities just because you are now a parent. And, it is not necessary to give up all opportunities, but it may be necessary to postpone some of them while you meet your obligations as a parent. Your child cannot be your only priority; both parents should and will accept other opportunities, but you need to make sure to pursue only the opportunities that are compatible with being available for your child, as you are needed.

By the time we are adults, we should have learned this basic truth: results are the product of the time and effort that we exert. That which we attend to and put our efforts toward, gets the results. That which we do not attend to can deteriorate. We can ignore our yard for a long time while we attend to more urgent things, knowing it will deteriorate and knowing that later we can go back, make it a priority, and take care of it so that it recovers. Or we can replace it and start over. Our children, however, cannot be ignored or replaced or even put on hold while we pursue other opportunities. If we continually ignore a child's needs, it may be extremely difficult, or impossible, to repair the damage later on. The time, energy, and money many parents spend trying to repair the damage to their child, far exceed what it would have taken to prevent the damage in the first place, by being available to help meet their child's needs before there was trouble.

Children are in a constant state of all kinds of development: physical, moral, spiritual, social, emotional, and intellectual. There are certain windows of opportunity for influencing children that may never come again. We can't even predict when the varied windows of opportunity may occur. Therefore, parents could not pick a chunk of

I Promise to Make You a Top Priority 23

time when it would be safe to ignore their children for a significant length of time.

Besides actually being a priority, children need to feel like a top priority. Most parents would tell us, "There is nothing in the world more important to me than my child." But if they don't function, on a regular basis, as if this is true, their child will not believe it. What a child sees you spending your time on appears to the child to be the most important to you.

Children may see many of their parents' interests—jobs, hobbies, TV, friends, church duties, the computer—take precedence over spending time with them. These children believe they are not valued by their parents as much as the interests that get more attention. They learn to feel unimportant and insignificant. They may learn to stay out of the way. Eventually, these children will not turn to their parents for attention or for guidance and advice when making critical decisions. These are the children who will turn to peers or even gangs to find a feeling of importance. They eventually make critical decisions based on what their peers say, rather than what their parents say.

Your child wants and needs your attention and affirmation even if he is not able to ask for it. Our children know that we all somehow find time for the things that simply must get done, the priorities. Children know they are a top priority when their parents show up at the school functions or other child-centered events, despite demanding schedules. When a child hears his parents turn down some adult function, to fulfill a promise made to the child, he knows he is an important priority.

One way for a very busy parent to make a child feel like a priority is to have a pre-scheduled "sacred time" each week that is devoted to doing something special, alone with just that child. When the parent can regularly keep that time sacred, forsaking outside offers or demands to change it, this is a powerful statement to the child that says "You are really important to me."

Making your child a priority now will pay off for you in your child's future, because children who have been made to feel like a priority have stronger self-images and fewer adjustment problems. Looking into your distant future, remember that how important you are to your children later in life, when you are old and need their attention, will definitely reflect just how important you made them feel as young children. To develop caring, generous, responsible children, you must make sure they know how valued they are, by making them a top priority in your life.

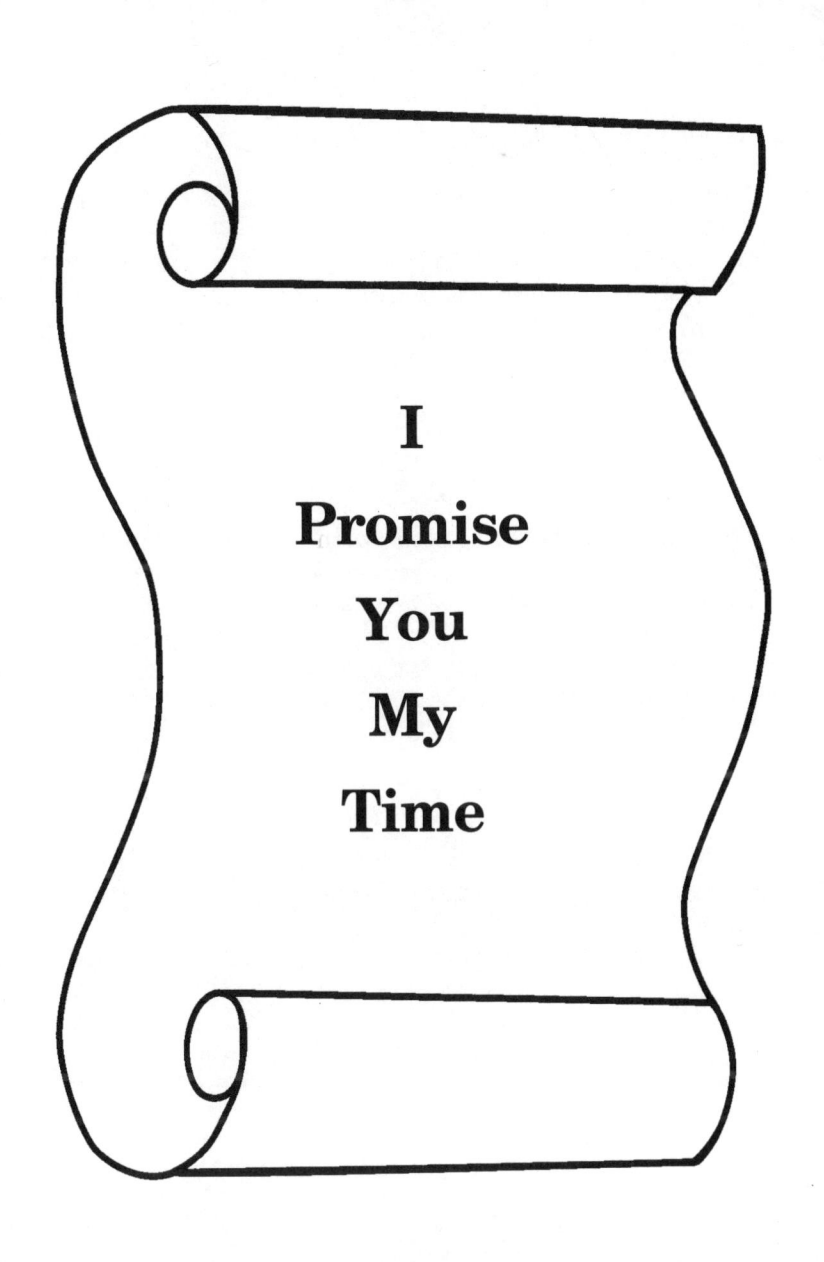

I Promise You My Time

IV

I Promise You My Time

Time is a very precious commodity these days, for all of us. Therefore, this may be one of the hardest promises to keep. But, next to absolute, unconditional love, the best gift you will ever give your child is your time. Your young child would rather play with you than with any toy or even any computer game that you could offer. For an example of this, watch a child's first few special occasions, opening a pile of gifts. You'll usually see him ignore the gifts, spend more time playing with the boxes and ribbon, and spend the most time trying to engage his parents' attention.

On the same special occasions, when you see the pile of gifts, think about the time it took his parents to: 1) earn the money to purchase the gifts; 2) decide on and then shop for the gifts; 3) wrap them; and 4) prepare for the celebration. Then see how much time each adult involved actually spends interacting with the children. In many cases the time spent on preparation efforts may have been more valuable if spent in simply playing with the children.

Any child, even a teenager, who receives desired and expensive gifts from parents who don't make time to spend with him, has little appreciation for the gift or the parents. The value of the gift, to the child, is more related to the value of the parent-child relationship than to the cost of the gift. Your attention is what makes your child feel valued.

Any child, but especially an infant, needs his parent's attention and his parent's reactions to provide clues and explanations of what he sees and hears. When the parent is there to react to a child's gestures, noises, movements, and comments, the parent's reinforcement helps the child make mental connections and construct new cognitive abilities. Quality communication between a child and the parent advances the child's cognitive and emotional development.

Our little ones need opportunities to play, and we as parents must provide that time. Busy parents who shuffle children around to fit pressing schedules need to arrange time for child's play. Play leads a child's development. Play introduces a child to regulatory activity, voluntary intentions, consideration of different perspectives, cooperation, goal setting, conflict resolution, planning, and creative expression. Even when it takes time, play should be a priority; for it is a child's work and should be treated with the respect it deserves.

Another reason to give your time to your children is that to know and understand anyone, you have to spend time around that person. You have to listen to, talk with, and observe the person often. By spending time with your child, you can really get to know him. By knowing him you will be better prepared to encourage him, praise him, teach him, and value him. You will be able to reinforce desired behaviors, set appropriate limits, and discipline effectively, according to his developmental needs.

Children learn primarily from the example of those whom they observe. So, as a parent, you need to think about who it is you want to be modeling behavior for your child: TV personalities; child-care providers; peers; certain relatives; or yourself. To instill the values, morals, and standards of behavior that you believe in, you need to be the one who is there, talking to and modeling for your child.

If you are so busy that you leave it to your spouse, or anyone else, to be the one who primarily cares for and relates to your child, you will lose out on many of the joys of watching your child develop and grow. And these are some of life's greatest moments. Moments that you can never get back. You will forfeit opportunities to share values and morals with your child. You may fail to establish the special bonding between parent and child that can enrich your life forever.

How much time is enough? Well, how much time do you spend on your career, travel, hobbies, TV, friends, sports, exercising? How can you budget your time? How much time can you give to each child? For stability and support, each child needs a significant percentage of your time along with your enthusiastic attention.

The time requirements vary as your child develops and his needs change. In the beginning years and then again in the adolescent years, the time demands are great. Parents simply must be available. If your children get used to your being there giving input when they are young, they are more likely to turn to you for advice when they reach those difficult years of puberty. Even if it seems they are pushing you away in those adolescent years, you need to be available, waiting in the wings for those critical periods of identity crisis, of questioning values, when, hopefully, they will seek you out for support and advice.

Part of the balancing act that every parent must perform depends on knowing when to get involved, when to intervene, and when to let the child fend for himself and learn from his choices. To know when and what to do, a parent has to be a conscientious observer of who the child is, what he is up against, and what he can manage on his own. Parents need to know when their six-year-old needs extra security and predictability, when their fourteen-year-old needs peer acceptance, and when their eighteen-year-old needs autonomy and validation. You can only make these observations by spending enough time with your child.

When we do make time to be with and guide our children, our advice and input as parents cannot come from our own life experiences alone. Our world growing up was vastly different from the world that our children experience. We may not accurately remember what our needs were at each stage. A fourteen-year-old today has different interests than a fourteen-year-old had 25 or 30 years ago. The assets and attributes for survival that your children will or will not develop are likely vastly different from the ones you had at the same age. Your advice and support, to be of value, needs to be based on knowledge of your child and familiarity with the challenges that he meets in today's society. You will not be able to gain this knowledge unless you spend a great deal of time with your child and unless you have opportunities for close observation of his life situations. These opportunities only come from spending time with your child.

I

Promise to

Listen

to

You

V

I Promise to Listen to You

To truly get to know another person, you have to listen to what that person has to say. If you listen attentively to your child, she will lead you to understand her perception of the world. To know her, to understand her, to really appreciate her perspective, you'll have to listen carefully and routinely. When you listen, without interrupting to lecture or give advice, you show respect for your child and you validate her feelings. This will make her feel important and valued.

To a parent, children can be the most delightful and insightful conversationalists. It would be a shame to miss what they have to offer, by not taking the time to listen carefully. You won't want to miss out on really getting to know who your child is and how she thinks throughout the different stages of her life. You'll want to be in on the entertaining and amazing insights unique to each delightful stage of development. You'll want to seize the opportunity to, once again, see the world through the innocent eyes of a child.

Listening is a vital part of building a positive, supportive relationship with anyone, the kind of relationship your child needs for healthy social, emotional, and cognitive development. When your child is very young, you are the primary means for fostering her language development. By talking to your child, you teach her the amazing patterns of language and how conversations work. By responding and reacting to her attempts to communicate, you help establish the patterns of verbal interaction that your child will take with her throughout her life.

When you see parents who have teenagers who still talk to them and share what's going on in their teenage lives, it's because the patterns of communication have been open for years. Those are the parents who have been listening to their children. Those are the teenagers who still listen to the advice their parents have to give. If you keep listening, your children will keep communicating with you, even through adolescence.

Children will not listen to adults who do not listen to them. If you want your children to listen to important information, such as your advice, your direction, or your values, you must listen to them when they have something to say. If you want to maintain opportunities to influence your children, you must believe what they have to say is important, beginning with the first babbles of baby talk. Treat what they have to say as important and, as the years go by, they will treat what you have to say as important.

You may be used to listening while you continue to stay busy cooking, working on the car, or half-watching TV. This is often not good enough when listening to your child, when she needs your full attention. She will not feel like you are listening unless you stop what you are doing and look her in the eye while she is talking. It is amazing how much more you will hear if all you are doing is listening. Even adults like to have others show us this respect when we are in a conversation. As you listen through the years, you will find it well worth the time it takes to stop everything else, look, and listen attentively to your child.

By being a good listener, you have an opportunity to model listening behaviors that you want your child to emulate. She will learn how to listen by your example. You will want your child to be a good listener because listening well is a skill that will give her an advantage in today's world. Television seems to have had a negative impact on listening skills for most of today's children. The visual presentation relieves us of the necessity of careful, attentive listening. The resulting careless listening skills make it difficult for many students to listen to instructions in school. The students who know how to actively listen have an advantage, because learning is easier for them.

To help guide your child toward better communication skills, you need to establish patterns of interaction in which you take turns listening and respecting each other's right to be heard. If you have so much to say yourself that you normally take over any conversation, resist the temptation to interrupt when listening to your child, and insist that she show you the same consideration. Each of you should get plenty of opportunity to share your views. By sharing and taking turns listening attentively, you will both learn more about each other while you perfect good communication skills.

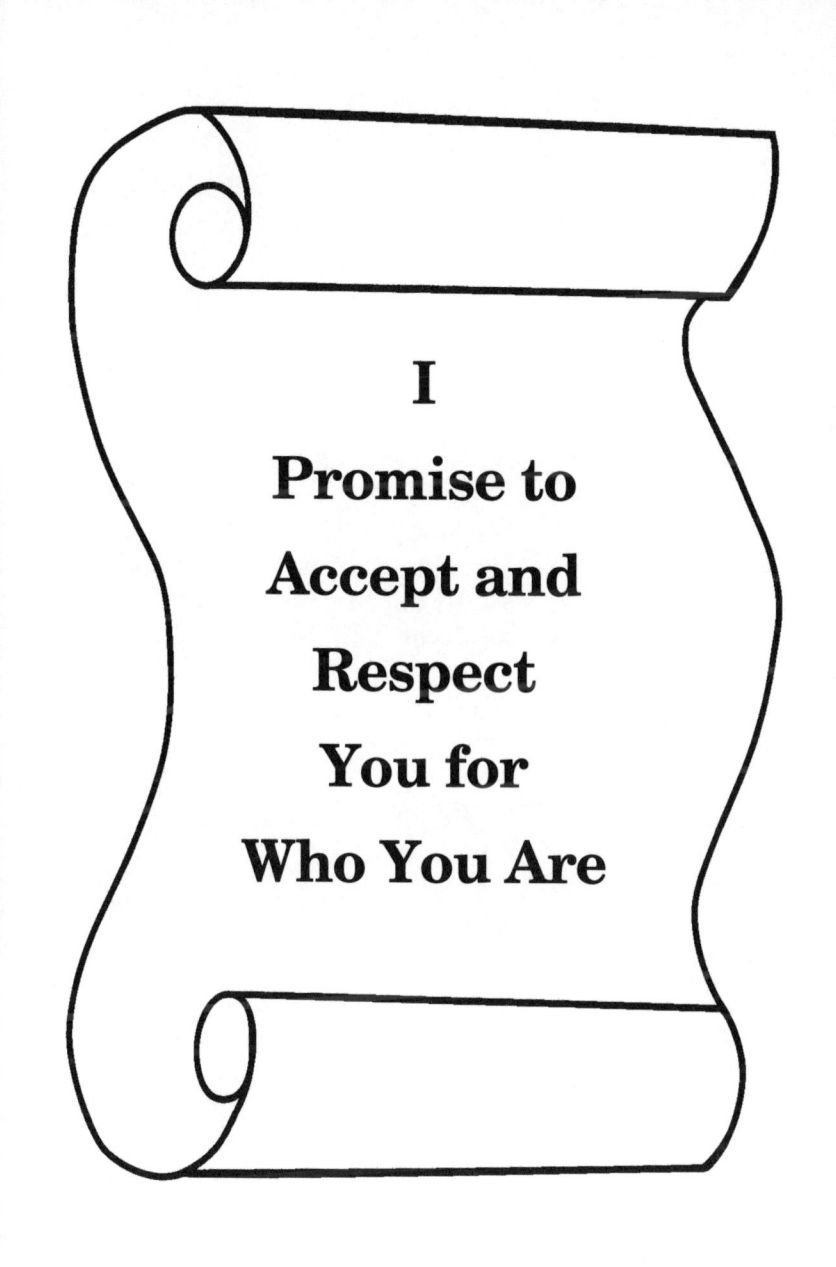

I Promise to Accept and Respect You for Who You Are

VI

I Promise to Accept and Respect You for Who You Are

Your precious child, like all children, is made up of a unique combination of attributes, strengths, and limitations. Each child deserves to be treasured for his uniqueness. What your child does with this unique combination of traits will somewhat depend on how he sees himself in relation to the rest of the people in his life. Discover your child's potential by focusing on and respecting his unique attributes and strengths. Help support your child in working around his limitations in order to minimize the effect they will have on his accomplishments.

How a child develops will depend on how his natural genetic makeup (physical, emotional, and intellectual) combines with everything that he experiences in life and how he reacts to those experiences. The uniqueness of each individual is created by this combination of natural makeup and environmental influence. Every child should be given support in learning how to make the most of his individual situation.

All areas of a child's development are influenced by the quality of his primary relationship with his parents. How you value your child will determine how he values himself for the rest of his life. To create and maintain a positive, caring, and loving relationship, you must make sure your child feels your acceptance and respect. Treat your child with the dignity that you show toward the adults whom you respect.

Accepting your child does not mean you have to accept every behavior. You need to make it perfectly clear when your child's behavior is inappropriate. But, at the same time, make sure you are also clear that it is the behavior, not the child, that is unacceptable. To have lasting positive influence on a child, you have to show him that you respect him even when you do not like certain behaviors. By making a distinction between the behaviors you do not like and acceptance of his uniqueness, you show respect for your child's feelings. He will be willing to listen to you, so you will continually have the opportunity to teach him appropriate reactions and better ways to handle life's situations.

Children who feel they are disappointing to their parents carry a great emotional burden. They feel incapable of pleasing and soon give up even trying to impress adults who are constantly

I Promise to Accept and Respect You for Who You Are 43

bringing up their shortcomings. When a child is treated like he is a disappointment, he will fall into a pattern of failures. He will never succeed as long as he is convinced he is a failure.

Criticism does not motivate most children to try harder. Success motivates and success begins with feeling valuable enough to succeed. To set your child up for success, make sure his challenges fit his ability. Children should only be asked to accomplish something that is within their grasp. When a child knows his parents believe in his ability and respect his individuality, he will be motivated to work toward proving he is worthy of this confidence in him.

Focus on your child's abilities and attributes without trying to mold him into your perception of who he should be. Your child should not be viewed as something to make you look good to others. Children should not be seen as a parent's second chance to get life right. We cannot expect our children to fulfill all of our lost dreams or succeed at that which we may have failed. Being unique individuals, as children develop, they will establish their own priorities and their own agendas. They need the freedom and support required to develop their potential in their own way.

In contrast to acceptance and respect for individuality in children, many adult agendas seem to be pressuring even very young children to perform up to some predetermined standard, both at home and at school. Many parents seem preoccupied with how their child makes them look as parents. These adults stress evaluating and comparing children to make sure their own measures up to some current notion of what children should be doing. Such approaches devalue individuality and rob children of their dignity. Don't let others put your child in the position of being compared or told they are inadequate by not meeting arbitrary standards.

Parents need to understand that adult preoccupation with how we look to others, how we measure up or compare, is not the preoccupation of children. Children are capable of finding great joy in just being and just experiencing, while they learn. If we allow them to develop at their own rate and to explore and learn without constantly having to prove themselves, they will find great joy in opportunities for growth. Children are here to develop and grow, not to be measured and evaluated to prove something to adults. Don't allow yourself to act disappointed in your child. Appreciate childhood as the valuable and unique stage of human development that it is.

The physical, emotional, moral, and intellectual development of a child takes years. They need those years because it takes time and patience for children to learn how to independently make good decisions and to solve problems successfully. They must have our acceptance, respect, and support along the way.

I Promise to Be Honest with You

VII

I Promise to Be Honest with You

Children are very smart little creatures, and extremely observant. Their eyes and ears work more efficiently than ours. Their active brains work much faster than ours. Therefore they are hard to fool. They are adept at figuring out the truth, and they are masters at reading their parents, so don't even try to get away with lying to your children. Children instinctively know when we are being honest with them, or when we are not.

It is never worth the risk to lie to, or around, your child because you will pay a very high price if you get caught, and the chances are you will get caught in the lie, by your child discovering the truth. Every time you are caught in a lie, your trustworthiness is diminished and your child's faith in you will deteriorate. You will teach them by example. Telling your children to be honest will not work if they see you being dishonest in your daily affairs.

There are certain exceptions to total honesty

that may very well be worth the risk. Most children eventually forgive their parents for misleading them for years about Santa, and the Easter Bunny. Children understand the use of such enjoyable fantasies and differentiate these fantasies from life's more self-serving lies. Also, children seem to learn quickly that unnecessary total honesty that insults or injures, such as telling a neighbor that he is ugly or stinky, is more damaging than a polite white lie meant to spare a person's feelings.

Otherwise, it is always best to be honest with and around your children if you want them to believe in you and trust you. To earn the respect of children, you must be honest with them. Respect is established when children learn to trust in you. Obviously we all have more respect for the people whom we know we can always believe.

Your example of honesty and integrity will determine how honest and honorable your child will become. We all are exposed to numerous lies every day from a variety of sources, such as advertisements and politics. Sometimes it seems we are all accepting lies as a necessary part of doing business. Many worry that our children will not find it necessary to be honest if they see national leaders being dishonest on a regular basis.

We may not expect the truth from politicians or salesmen, but we still do expect it from our children. Exposure to lies outside of the child's personal circle of influence will probably not turn him into a liar. But, if children see their parents lie to others on a regular basis, they will likely also lie. Besides losing respect for their parents when they hear them lie, children will lose respect for the truth. Without respect for the truth, they will feel free to be dishonest themselves. Children who are not taught the value of honesty lie to their parents as well as others. Not only do you want your children to believe in you, but you also want them to honor truthfulness throughout life so that others will respect and trust them for their honesty.

A pattern of honesty is essential between a parent and a child if you are to maintain a positive influence on the child's life. If your children learn to trust you about ordinary everyday life issues, they will be able to believe you when you say illegal drugs are dangerous, ignoring traffic laws can kill you, or teenage sex is too risky. Teenagers who listen to their parents about these important issues have learned to trust their parents because honesty has been a part of their relationship through their years together. The patterns of an honest relationship must be both long term and consistent.

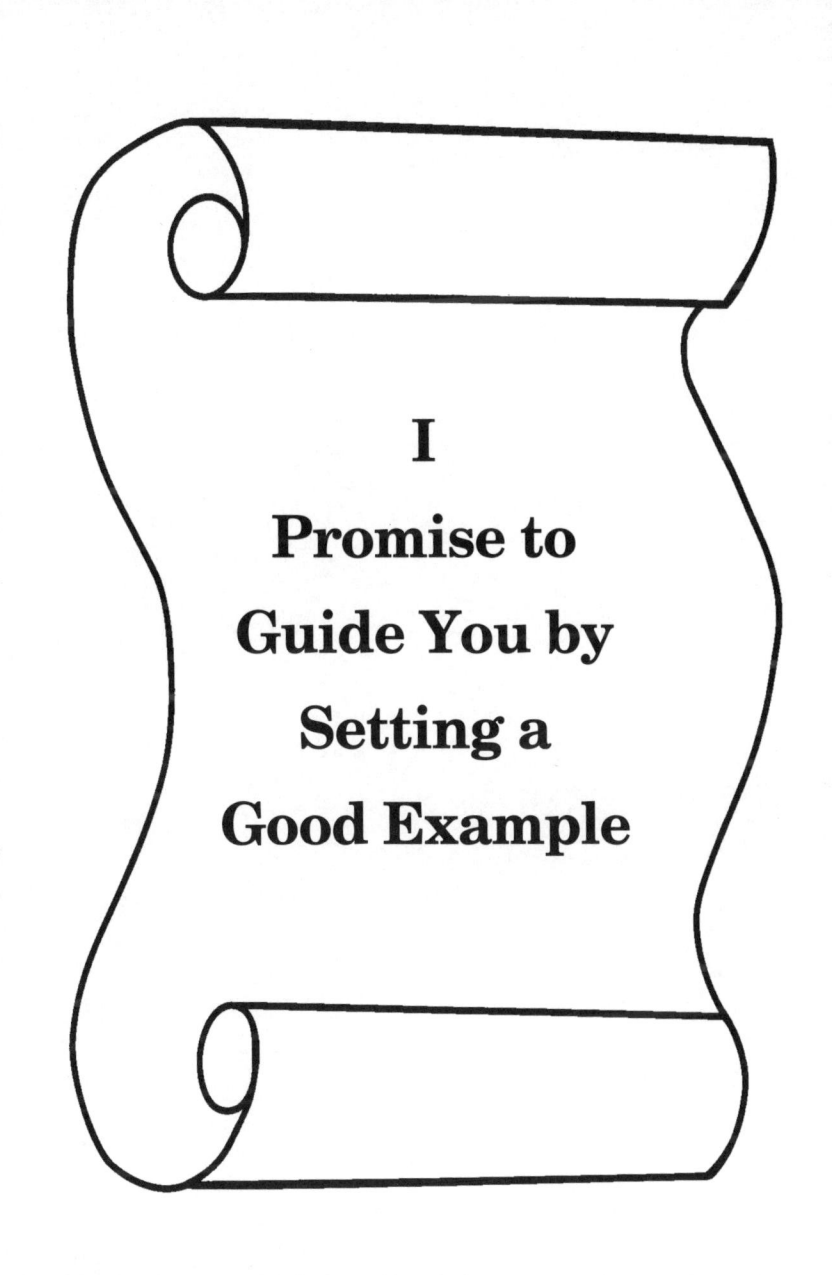

I
Promise to Guide You by Setting a Good Example

VIII

I Promise to Guide You by Setting a Good Example

Of all the influences in your child's life, you as the parent will have the greatest opportunity to impact your child's beliefs and values. But not by what you say, rather by what you do.

You will have the most powerful influence on your child during his earliest years. Luckily, in these early formative years, you will have more opportunities for input than your child's peers and the rest of the outside world. The early years are when all experiences and observations, along with your child's genetic makeup, will set up his basic patterns of thinking, basic ways of reacting, and basic personality traits. Being there and being available to influence your child during these crucial formative years is essential if you want to impact his value system. Never again, after the first few years, will you have as much of your child's undivided attention. Later on you may have very little control over all the examples set for your child.

The values and beliefs you want your child to adopt must be modeled by your behavior. Sorry, there is no other way. If you don't want your child to lie, cheat, or steal, you must not lie, cheat, or steal. If you do not want your child to criticize, ridicule, or bully others, he must not see you criticize, ridicule, or bully other people. If you want your child to treat other people with dignity and respect, he has to see you living with respect and dignity toward others, especially family members.

The cooperation established at home can determine your child's ability to work with others in and outside of the home. How parents treat each other has a major influence on how their children relate to others. How siblings interact is often a reflection of how their parents interact. By watching you make mistakes, disagree, and problem-solve with your spouse, your children will learn how it is done. Constructive conflict resolution skills are first developed in the home.

The simple notion that children learn from example is one we have all heard before, but it is often ignored by parents. These parents may act shocked by inappropriate behaviors in their children, when others, close to the situation, may have observed the same behaviors in the parents for years. These close observers are not in the

I Promise to Guide You by Setting a Good Example 57

least bit shocked to see it in the children because it is strikingly similar to the behaviors of their parents.

Sometimes, however, we do see behaviors in children that are completely foreign to the parent's behaviors. Parents who have not established a strong bond of communication and mutual respect with their children may find their children operating with a value system completely opposed to that of their parents. Parents who have lived according to very strict moral codes often find their children have not adopted the same standards. A stronger, more trusting relationship between the parents and the child may have resulted in more similar values.

On the other hand, fortunately, a child with parents who seem to have no morals can grow up to develop strong morals, if influenced by other more moral adults the child has had an opportunity to get to know and respect. Children are exposed to a multitude of examples of behavior that can have a huge impact on the development of their value systems. Children will emulate people whom they feel some sort of attachment to, people they can identify with.

Obviously, you are not the only influence on your child. Anyone a child spends time with models behavior that your child may or may not imitate. For a period of time, parents can choose who will be around their children to have influence. If you know of relatives, friends, or others who will be modeling undesirable behaviors for your children, make sure to limit the exposure or, if it is unavoidable, at least discuss it with your children to explain how you view the behaviors.

Since the adults in our society, or even adults within a family, no longer agree about what is appropriate behavior, your children will hear many different opinions. Make sure they hear yours. You have to help your children learn to make choices about how to act. Communicate your beliefs openly and often without being oppressive. Even when children do not seem to be listening, what you say does have an impact, if they respect you. First they must see you live according to your standards and demonstrate how your standards benefit your life.

Your child will most assuredly be exposed to alternative values and beliefs, values and beliefs that can scare a parent into paranoia. No matter how much we would like to, today's parents have no hope of insulating their children from this exposure to alternative ideas, even with home schooling or restricting the movies they see. Alternative values are everywhere in our society. But, how much influence this inevitable exposure to undesirable values will have on your child depends a great deal on how much respect your child has for you. With strong consistent role modeling and a strong loving bond between parent and child, outside negative influences have less power to persuade.

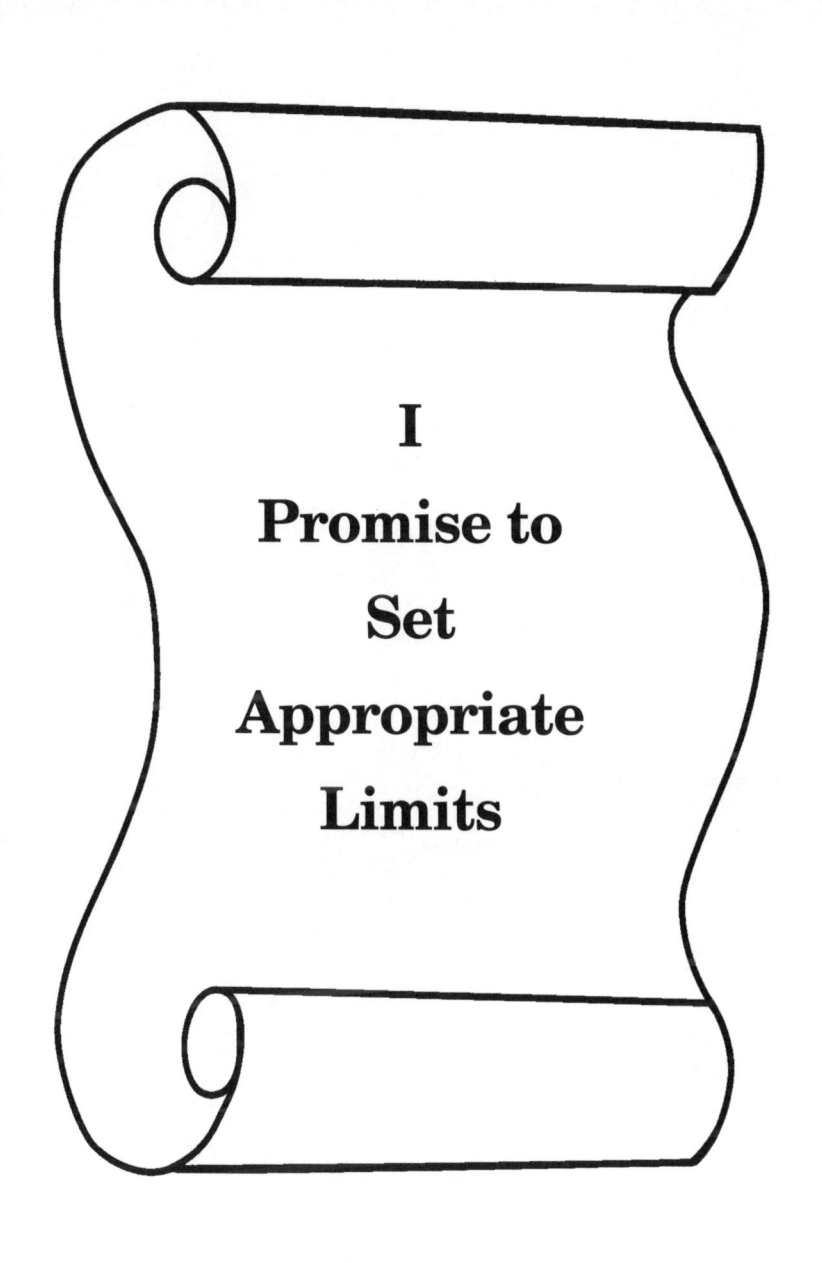

I
Promise to
Set
Appropriate
Limits

IX

I Promise to Set Appropriate Limits

Children feel, and actually are, more secure when parents provide adequate structure and establish boundaries, boundaries that are adjusted to the child's developmental needs. For children, appropriate limits help build self-control, responsibility, confidence, problem-solving skills, integrity, independence, and respect for others.

Children are smart enough to know they must depend on adults. They instinctively know they are not equipped to be in charge, even though they may be acting like they want all the control. Even though they argue and seem to reject limits, it actually makes children feel more secure when the adults demonstrate confidence and ability in establishing rules regarding sensible boundaries.

Whatever the stage of development, most activities that children enjoy have to have some limit attached: playing in the sun; watching TV; exploring physical feats; playing video games; eating junk food; hanging around with peers; exploring new freedoms. It is the parents' responsibility to pay attention to the risks and establish safe parameters for their children.

It is often easier for a parent to give in to a child's demands than it is to go through the hassle of setting and enforcing limits. However, because of the benefits to the child of having limits, it can be considered parental neglect to fail to set limits. Besides making your life miserable, overindulgence sends out wrong messages to your child: "rules are arbitrary," "anything goes if I want it bad enough," "my wants are more important than the rights and needs of others." Children who do not learn how to function within limits, set by respected authority figures, have a tough time adjusting to school, succeeding in sports, participating in competitions, cooperating in organizations, or keeping a job.

Limits help children figure out how the real world works so they can function productively in society. In a world full of so many people working on so many agendas, it is not possible for any of us to survive without recognizing and accepting certain limits. Eventually children need to learn how to set appropriate boundaries internally. To prepare to do this, they first must learn to accept and adjust to limits set externally by caring adults. Children need to learn, in the safe environment of home, what all can result when they defy limits

I Promise to Set Appropriate Limits 65

and have to face the consequences. They need to experience the benefits of making responsible decisions.

An important aspect of setting appropriate limits is to consider your child's age and developmental level. Consider what she can do independently and what all she needs to be challenged. Consider what is required for her to be safe, successful, and happy. Within the parameters of safety, allow children to make choices that you can all live with.

Effective discipline offers guidance by letting the child know exactly what is expected and what the consequences will be if she ignores those expectations. Both expectations and consequences need to remain consistent as long as they make sense. By understanding expectations and the possible consequences of their choices, children develop the ability to make better decisions for the rest of their lives. By experiencing consequences of their own decisions, children gain knowledge about such relationships as cause and effect, effort and results, neglect and pain. Children learn how to control themselves safely, which leads to increased self-confidence.

In contrast to giving children choices within safe limits, rigid, unrealistic, adult-imposed rules, followed by severe punishment when broken, are not as effective in developing autonomy and responsible self-control in children. Engaging in endless power struggles with children is not part of effective discipline. It only sharpens a child's skills in arguing with parents, defending, griping, criticizing, accusing, being hostile, passively complying or avoiding responsibility. As a parent you will want to establish more positive and more productive coping skills in your children, such as accountability, responsibility, reliability, adaptability, and creative problem-solving.

Success will be more likely if your limits and expectations are simple, positively stated, and easy to follow. To set such limits, parents need to be aware of what behaviors, skills, and desires are to be expected for the developmental stage of their child. You will have to have some knowledge of the stages of child development and what the needs are for each stage. This information is available in a variety of materials throughout schools, libraries, the medical community, and the media.

When limits are challenged, living with the consequences can teach children powerful lessons. Positive learning is more likely if rational and appropriate consequences are dealt with in a calm, fair, but firm manner. Once the consequences have occurred, let it be finished, with no nagging to remind the child of her mistake. You don't want her to focus on the nagging. You want her to focus

I Promise to Set Appropriate Limits 67

on how her choices led to the natural consequences.

Children need to be allowed a fresh start, the chance to succeed next time, without lingering expectations of failure or repeated disappointment. Always express your expectation that your child will accept the appropriate limits the next time she gets to make a choice. Let your child know you expect her to make good choices. Let her know you think she can handle decisions. The limits, choices, mistakes, natural consequences, and fresh starts will help your child learn self-discipline and responsibility. The sooner a child learns how to make good decisions within appropriate limits, the more pleasant your lives will be.

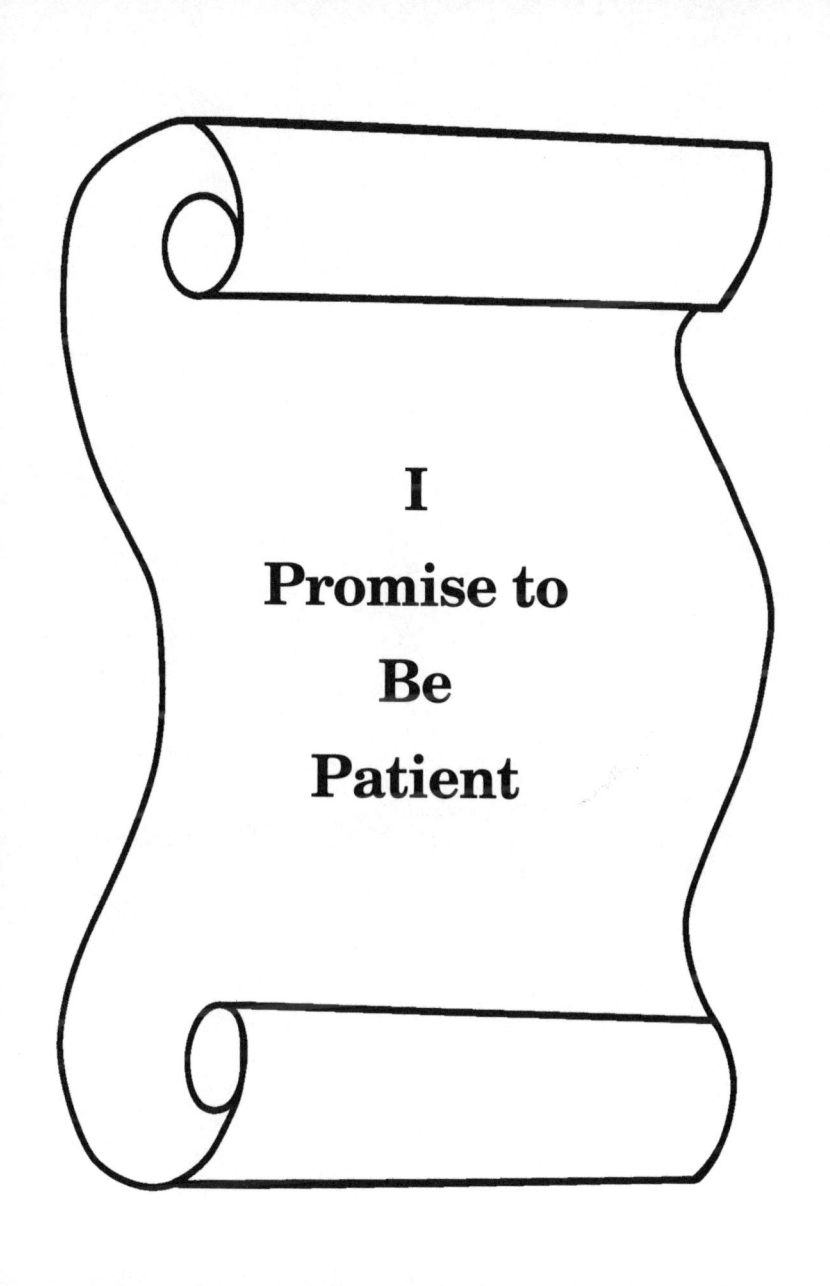

I

Promise to

Be

Patient

X

I Promise to Be Patient

Let's face it, we are not all patient people. Furthermore, it is a difficult trait to establish if you are not naturally endowed with the quality. Yet, to be a parent, you simply must learn patience. To do this job right, to do right by children, takes tons of patience along with hours and hours of commitment. So if you are to become a parent, first become patient. And hurry up about it! Your children will need your patience from the very beginning.

Children are not to be rushed in everyday efforts. Rushing a child usually has opposite the desired effect; it slows them down. Patience is needed because children learn by doing things for themselves, yet it takes more time to let a child do anything or clean up any mess than it would take you to just do it yourself. Patient parents allow their children the time and trouble it takes to benefit from each experience and gain responsibility.

The development of a child takes many years

of patience. Most other animals on earth become independent within a year or two. Our babies are designed to develop slowly and must be cared for patiently along this slow process. Even though we may try to rush the developmental process for our own convenience, it cannot be rushed without consequences. Childhood takes a long time, and that's a good thing. Be patient and enjoy it while it lasts.

Unfortunately for our children, our society is changing in such a way as to rob many children of the nurturing and care needed by a loving, patient parent because so many parents are working long hours outside of the home soon after the baby is born. Many infants and toddlers are having to fend for themselves in day-care facilities while older children may be spending hours at home, alone, waiting for their parents to return from work. Maybe this is part of the reason our ideas about childhood are changing. We seem to be trying to convince ourselves that our children really do need early exposure to socialization and readiness skills provided by institutions and really do not need a parent around all that much.

The troubles our children are having with learning, the decline in respect for adults, the growing numbers of children who are overweight or anorexic, the increase in identified childhood disabilities (such as attention deficit disorder), the number of children on medication, and the horrors of youth violence, should all be convincing us that our children are not getting what they need from the adults in this society. Adults today are too busy and too stressed to be patient with childhood. Not enough of us are enjoying the childhood years of our children.

Parents are signing their children up for a variety of structured, organized activities at a younger and younger age: music lessons, sports camps, pre-school computer classes, private tutoring, dance lessons, self-defense classes, or just about anything offered. Maybe it is to keep them busy while the parents attend to other pursuits, maybe it is to get some relief from the stress of being a parent. Most say it is to help their children develop skills and to get ahead in a competitive society. Whatever the reason, there seems to be a trend of rushing our younger children into activities way before they have developed the personal skills to cope with all the demands for performance.

In individual homes, impatient parents are rushing their children to master each new task early: walking, talking, reading, writing, swimming, playing an instrument, computer skills, etc. It is like we want to ensure their success by seeing that they can accomplish each skill as early as possible. "If I can see my child doing it right now, I don't have to worry about them being able to accomplish this later, at the more expected time."

Maybe some parents believe the sooner we get them to act like little adults, the sooner we can quit feeling guilty about not being with them as often as we would like. Maybe, through their child's accomplishments, parents are seeking affirmation that they have not messed up their child by not being available. Parents do not seem to realize that by pushing their children to accomplish things for which they are not ready, they run the risk of making their children feel inadequate and disappointing. They run the risk of mutilating the joys of childhood. They run the risk of ruining their relationship with their children.

Obviously children can benefit from opportunities such as music lessons, sports camps, and other enrichment classes, when they are old enough to handle such situations. But they also need some unstructured time to just be kids, to learn on their own, to create their own entertainment and their own fascinations, to get to know and understand themselves. Even when children are older, there needs to be a balance between structured activities that demand performance toward accomplishment and unstructured, yet supervised, activities that allow children freedom of choice and some self-regulation. It is easier to sign them up for activities that turn your child's supervision over to other adults, but parents need to find the time and patience to offer the balance needed, to give your children opportunities to just be kids.

If you study all of the developmental milestones of childhood at each age level, it becomes apparent that children need a parent's loving support, time, and attention in order to accomplish all that is required to emerge into healthy, functioning individuals. To develop a healthy self-concept, children need to be appreciated for who they are and what they can do at each stage, recognized for their little accomplishments along the way. As children develop in different ways along the way, each at their own individual pace, they need to be encouraged and supported for their efforts. Someone with patience and understanding needs to be there for each child, to inspire effort and recognize potential. Children need numerous opportunities for discovery and success that only a patient parent can insure.

I Promise to Protect You

XI

I Promise to Protect You

For children to achieve healthy physical, emotional, spiritual, and cognitive development, they must feel protected and safe. To provide a safe environment for your child is not as simple as locking up the poisons or providing protection from the criminals. A safe environment also means having an emotionally healthy home, free of ridicule, degradation, and abuse of any kind.

A child must be protected from all harmful influences to the body, mind, or spirit. To protect your children, it is essential to provide an environment that is non-threatening. Any domestic violence or verbal abuse between adults is threatening to a child and will impact the child's development. The tension of marital problems between parents cannot be hidden from the children, so it is imperative that parents work to solve conflicts constructively, seeking outside professional help if needed.

If either parent is debilitated or consumed by

an addiction of any kind, their children will suffer. Parents cannot afford to ignore such problems. In the interest of their children, parents need to resolve such addictive and destructive behaviors.

As a parent you need to protect your children from those who can do harm of any kind. More often than the boogie man or the perverts, your child may be exposed to so-called responsible influences that could do less obvious harm, like relatives, friends, baby-sitters, teachers, day-care providers, religious instructors, coaches, or Scout leaders. If any of these people belittle or humiliate children, do not trust them around yours. To protect your children, you cannot be blindly trusting of those whose job it is to help children.

If unsupervised, your children could be exposed to a steady diet of undesirable characters on television or through other forms of the media. It is the parent's job to monitor what your child watches or listens to for as long as you have such control. As your children age, you will have less and less to say about what they are exposed to. You can't be there all the time.

You will sometimes have to protect your children from what you do. If your children see you watching or reading something appropriate for adults only (or not appropriate for anybody), they will be curious and want to see it also. You may simply have to veto certain programs, video games, movies, or magazines from your home. Let your children observe you reading books. Interact with them by playing a game instead of depending on mass media for most of your entertainment.

Part of protecting your children includes teaching them at an early age how to be cautious and how to protect themselves from harm. Children need to learn how to be assertive with peers and to say no when it is appropriate, even to people in positions of authority. Teaching your children dependence and blind obedience without reason can make them vulnerable targets. Encourage their inner strength and independence of mind.

As children age, they spend increasing time away from their parents and in today's world unacquainted adults in the community usually do not get involved with children to the extent of looking out for them. This makes it important for you to establish friendships with trustworthy adults who can become part of your child's protective world. Children need to know how to get help and whom to turn to when they need it. For the times when you are not available your children need to know there are other adults they can trust.

I
Promise to Help You Develop Independence

XII

I Promise to Help You Develop Independence

It is a long slow road to independence for human babies, but it is a continuous road that begins as soon as they are born. Children are so dependent on parents at first that we can get quite used to being needed and to having total control. As our little ones develop toward self-reliance, it can be difficult to let go, but it is essential to stand back and let our children gain independence as they are able to handle it.

Welcome your child's development of self-confidence by celebrating her achievements toward independence. This encouragement builds the self-reliance that every child will need in order to thrive. Independent thinking skills are necessary for children to be able to develop higher order problem-solving strategies needed in their education and in life. As your child develops independence, she gains confidence and the personal inner strength needed to cope with any hardships that life may present.

A child's road to self-assurance and eventual self-reliance begins early. Before your child enters school much of her brain development has already occurred and the ultimate learning rate has already happened. The variety of sights, sounds, smells and touching that the infant experiences combine to form lasting impressions of the world. The pre-school years are critical to your child's future development. Everything you do with your child is a learning experience that builds brain connections to create foundations for future learning.

Normal everyday interactions between you and your child, beginning in the infant years, provide the building blocks for future learning. Talking to your child and reading to her have significant impact on the development of language skills, and later, on her reading ability. Play activities that involve sorting, arranging, stacking, sequencing, and organizing toys, establish foundations for understanding of math and science concepts later on. Allowing your infant to explore independently, fall down, and make mistakes allows her to discover processes of recovery. Such experiences allow her to make connections between cause and effect, between choices and consequences.

Once they are in school, help your children establish a respect for education and for educators by supporting them in school and in school activities. Make education a priority in your home by modeling your own continuing life-long learning. Help establish a routine schedule for doing homework every evening, or for quiet thinking time if no homework is assigned. Provide a consistent location for doing homework and a peaceful, quiet environment that's conducive to concentration. Teach them how to help themselves and how to be personally accountable for their work.

If your child is not feeling successful in school, be proactive and get in there to figure out what the problem is. All children would rather be successful in school if they had the choice. Children are not choosing to fail. There is always some reason for school failure, some reason the child feels is beyond her control. When given the needed support and shown how to succeed, children will succeed. They differ on how much and what kind of support they need. So, if your child is not succeeding in school, go in and find out what changes need to be made. Discover how she can be better supported at home and at school. Find out if special interventions are needed. Don't allow your children to simply blame others for their school problems. Help them learn to look for solutions to school problems. Help empower your children by showing them how to problem solve, take responsibility, and be accountable.

An effective way to give your child an educational advantage over other children is to limit her time in front of the TV or computer. Everyone in your home needs some quiet, alone time every day, just a chance to think on their own, without outside input from other people or the media. With limited access to external entertainment children learn to use their brains in more productive ways, developing cognitive skills to create their own amusements. Once developed, creative thinking skills lead to higher achievement in school and throughout life. People who can think for themselves, people who can create their own fun, are less dependent and happier individuals.

Help your children become excited about all learning by providing multiple learning experiences in the home and the community. Expose them to art and good music. Take the family to the zoo, the library, cultural events, museums and historical sites. Play a variety of games with your children. Games provide multiple interactive learning opportunities.

It is naive and irresponsible to expect the schools to take total responsibility of your child's education. No school, including expensive private schools, can give your child all the education that she needs, because much of what we need to know

I Promise to Help You Develop Independence 89

cannot be taught in school, but must be experienced out in the real world. Parents have to get back to accepting responsibility for much of their child's education. Share your hobbies, skills, and special interests with your child. Offer her opportunities to help you with daily responsibilities such as cooking, house cleaning, shopping, changing the oil, yard work, planning family outings, caring for animals, or balancing the checkbook.

Encourage independence even if it means your child is more of a challenge to control. If parents discourage independence, their children can begin to feel guilty about growth and accomplishments. They may begin to avoid effort or development of new skills and abilities. We can enjoy those first few years, when our little ones totally depend on us, for a while. But when the warm feelings of being needed cause us to do too much for our children, as they become more capable, we send the wrong message. Doing too much for children sends messages that say we aren't sure they can handle life. By causing self-doubts we are in danger of delaying development and limiting their achievements.

For development of healthy self-esteem, all children need opportunities for accomplishment both in school and outside of school. They need to learn how their own personal effort can lead to rewarding accomplishments. Help your children find interests and activities in which they can excel. Self-esteem is developed by using one's ability to accomplish something worthwhile. Require your children to be totally responsible for certain chores as part of their development of life skills in responsibility, cooperation, and problem solving. Successfully executed chores help build confidence and an appreciation for other people's efforts.

As you offer educational experiences and opportunities for accomplishment you help your child build character and develop independence. You help prepare your child for handling life's many challenges successfully. In addition, your child will achieve the awareness that you care enough to spend the time and effort that it takes to help her develop and grow toward independence.

Final Comments

Honoring your child with a loving relationship, by promising a standard of quality interactions as outlined in this book, will enhance your relationship while helping your child develop the inner strength needed to face the challenges of life. This strength is immediately apparent in children who have been so honored by their parents.

When you see children who have a strong, dignified relationship with their parents, they stand out. These children look happy. They have pep, energy, and enthusiasm for life. They are free of the emotional burdens that many other children carry. These children can handle life's challenges with an inner strength. They may have a variety of ability levels and even have disabilities to contend with, but they still exude a certain confidence and maintain a motivation to work toward goals. They look and act like *children,* exploring life with creativity and charm. They relate well to others and usually have a variety of friends. These kids are enjoyable to be around.

The Twelve Parent Promises will not necessarily insulate your child from all problems. The complex issues children face today cannot be escaped, no matter what you do. You cannot completely prevent exposure to undesirable influences throughout your child's life. However, through honorable interactions, we can develop bonds with our children that will strengthen their resistance and make them less vulnerable to dangerous influences. We can give them tools with which to handle problems and conflicts. We can teach them to cope with the distresses of life without letting sadness take over.

By keeping the Twelve Parent Promises whenever possible, you will be giving your children the level of support needed to make the most of their personal assets. You will be giving them support needed to better deal with life's challenges. By providing a positive climate of spiritual well-being in your home, you can prevent many problems that could sabotage the healthy development of your child's character. You will strengthen your child for life.

As a society we need to realize the importance of adequate parenting. It will determine the well-being of our children and therefore the quality of our future. We must find ways to help all parents prepare for raising children, ideally before they become parents. As there are standards for education and standards in industry, there must be standards for parenting.

Our society needs to get back to cherishing our children. Only by cherishing them will we produce children who are delightful to be around, children who are capable of reaching their own potential. As a parent, you can do your part by keeping these Twelve Parent Promises to your own children. By doing so, you will model effective parenting for others and you will help train your own children to be great parents in the future.

Keeping these twelve essential Parent Promises will provide you the opportunity to establish a relationship of immense quality with your child, which will provide you with limitless personal satisfaction. You will enjoy your years of parenting. Both you and your children will have those years to remember fondly for the rest of your lives. Living by such high standards of relating constitutes mutual respect. If you keep these promises, you will earn your child's trust, love, and emulation for life. Your child will be strong and capable.

Bibliography

Benson, Peter L., Galbraith, Judy & Espeland, Pamela. (1995). *What Kids Need to Succeed: Proven, practical ways to raise good kids.* Minneapolis, MN: Free Spirit Publications.

Berk, Laura, E. & Winsler, Adam. (1995). *Scaffolding Children's Learning: Vygotsky and early childhood education.* Washington, DC: National Association for the Education of Young Children.

Bredekamp, Sue & Copple, Carol, Editors. (1997). *Developmentally Appropriate Practice in Early Childhood Programs* (Revised Ed.). Washington, DC: National Association for the Education of Young Children.

Brooks, Robert. (1991). *The Self-Esteem Teacher: Seeds of self-esteem.* Circle Pines, MN: American Guidance Service.

Cline, Foster & Fay, Jim. (1990). *Parenting with Love and Logic: Teaching children responsibility.* Colorado Springs, CO: Navpress.

Clinton, Hillary Rodham. (1996). *It Takes a Village: And other lessons children teach us.* New York: Simon & Schuster.

Collins, Marva & Tamarkin, Civia. (1982). *Marva Collins's Way: Return to excellence.* Los Angeles: Jeremy P. Tarcher, Inc.

Coloroso, Barbara. (1989). *Winning at Parenting . . . without beating your kids* (video). (From the series "Kids Are Worth It," P.O. Box 621108, Littleton, CO 80162.)

Dinkmeyer Sr., Don, McKay, Gary D., & Dinkmeyer, James S. (1989). *Parenting Young Children: Helpful strategies based on Systematic Training for Effective Parenting (STEP) for parents of children under six.* Circle Pines, MN: American Guidance Service.

Elkind, David. (1988). *The Hurried Child.* Reading, MA: Addison-Wesley.

Gardner, Howard. (1983). *Frames of Mind: The theory of multiple intelligences.* New York: Basic Books, Inc.

Ginott, Haim G. (1972). *Teacher & Child.* New York: Avon Books.

Goleman, Daniel. (1995). *Emotional Intelligence: Why it can matter more than IQ.* New York: Bantam Books.

Gordon, Thomas. (1976). *P.E.T. in Action: The newest most complete guide to parent effectiveness training.* New York: Bantam Books.

Healy, Jane M. (1990). *Endangered Minds.* New York: Touchstone, Simon & Schuster.

Healy, Jane M. (1987). *Your Child's Growing Mind: A*

practical guide to brain development and learning from birth to adolescence (2nd ed.) New York: Doubleday.

Kagan, Jerome. (1998). *Three Seductive Ideas.* Cambridge, MA: Harvard University Press.

Kagan, Jerome. (1998). *Galen's Prophecy,* Boulder, CO: Westview Press.

Kagan, Jerome. (1984). *The Nature of the Child.* New York: Basic Books.

Levine, Melvin D. (1987). *Developmental Variation and Learning Disorders.* Cambridge, MA: Educators Publishing Service, Inc.

Reinert, Henry R. & Huang, Allen. (1987). *Children in Conflict.* (3rd ed.) Columbus: Merrill Publishing.

Rimm, Sylvia B. (1986). *Underachievement Syndrome: Causes and Cures.* Watertown, WI: Apple Publishing.

Rimm, Sylvia B. (1990). *How to Parent So Children Will Learn.* Watertown, WI: Apple Publishing.

Salkind, Neil J. (1981). *Theories of Human Development* (2nd Ed.) New York: Wiley & Sons.

Starr, Constance & Starr, William. (1983). *To Learn with Love: A companion for Suzuki Parents,* Knoxville, TN: Kingston Ellis Press.

The Greeley Dream Team. (1995). *First and Foremost: Understanding parenting and effective skills to raise your children* (video series, volumes 1-20). (Available from Weld County School District 6

Media Services, 2508 Fourth Avenue, Greeley, CO 80631.)

Weissbourd. (1996). *The Vulnerable Child: What really hurts America's children and what we can do about it.* Reading, MA: Addison-Wesley.

Wertsch, James V. (1991). *Voices of the Mind: A sociocultural approach to mediated action.* Cambridge, MA: Harvard University Press.